THE OTHER

THE OTHER

RYSZARD KAPUŚCIŃSKI

Translated by Antonia Lloyd-Jones
with an introduction by Neal Ascherson

VERSO
London • New York

INSTYTUT KSIĄŻKI

©POLAND

This publication has been subsidized by Instytut Książki
© POLAND translation programme

This edition published by Verso 2008
© Ryszard Kapuściński 2006
Translation © Antonia Lloyd-Jones 2008
First published as Ten Inny © Wydawnicto Znak, Kraków 2006
1 3 5 7 9 10 8 6 4 2

Verso
UK: 6 Meard Street, London W1F 0EG
USA: 20 Jay Street, Brooklyn, NY 11201
www.versobooks.com

Verso is the imprint of New Left Books

ISBN-13: 978-1-84467-328-5

British Library Cataloguing in Publication Data
A catalogue record for this book is available from the British Library

Library of Congress Cataloging-in-Publication Data
A catalog record for this book is available from the Library of Congress

Typeset by Hewer Text UK Ltd, Edinburgh
Printed in the USA by Maple Vail

CONTENTS

The subject of the lectures collected in this volume is the Other. They were delivered as follows:

'Viennese Lectures' (I, II, III), 1–3 December 2004, at the Institut für die Wissenschaften vom Menschen in Vienna;

'My Other', 12 October 1990, at the International Writers' Symposium in Graz;

'The Other in the Global Village', 30 September 2003, during the inauguration of the academic year at the Father Józef Tischner Senior European School in Kraków;

'Encountering the Other as the Challenge of the Twenty-First Century', 1 October 2004, on the occasion of being awarded the title of doctor *honoris causa* at the Jagiellonian University in Kraków.

R. K.

INTRODUCTION

Towards the end of this book, Kapuściński quotes the great Polish-born pioneer of social anthropology, Bronisław Malinowski. In his book *Argonauts of the West Pacific*, Malinowski wrote that 'to judge something, you have to be there'.[1]

It's a contestable generalisation. It's obvious that, of those who passed judgements on the nature of the Hitler or Stalin regimes, and who often perished in the effort to enforce those judgements, extremely few had literally 'been there'. However, Malinowski's line is an indispensable motto for all good journalists. The late Ryszard Kapuściński followed it throughout his career, pursued it indeed to extremes of danger and isolation which few of

---

1. B. Malinowski, *Argonauts of the Western Pacific: An Account of Native Enterprise and Adventure in the Archipelagoes of Melanesian New Guinea*, Studies in Economics and Political Science, no. 65, London: Routledge & Kegan Paul, 1922.

his colleagues ventured to endure. Did he really have to find himself awaiting execution in a dirty African cell in order to judge the politics of Congolese independence? No, but he added to his ability to judge fear and humiliation and – because he got out of that cell – to describe the sudden savour of life after the expectation of death.

His most famous book, *The Emperor*, also demonstrates the importance of 'being there', in that case settling in Addis Ababa in order to seek out and interview the surviving courtiers of the fallen Haile Selassie.[2] It should be added that Kapuściński understands 'being there' as requiring a dimension in time as well as space. It's strange to recall that for much of his life he was an agency journalist, often subject to the insane pressure of deadlines and call-backs and updates at any hour of the day or night. His instinct, in complete contrast, was to stop the clock and let people take all the hours and days they needed to disentangle, unwind and lay out their story. This is what he did in *The Emperor*, whose enquiries seem to take place across weeks and months, as well as in dark lanes and shuttered houses.

Kapuściński is usually remembered in Western Europe and America as an iconic foreign correspondent and as the writer of narratives about his experiences in Africa,

2. R. Kapuściński, *The Emperor: Downfall of an Autocrat*, London: Penguin Classics, 2006.

Latin America and Asia, which were famous for their often surreal imagery, their revelations of misery and cruelty, and the fastidious quality of their writing. He was certainly a king at his craft, and also a brave, witty man who could be a good comrade in the field. A question often raised about him later in his career, but never convincingly answered, was where – in him – the frontier between literature and reporting ran. It's a hard one to answer, not least because there is no such wire barrier (floodlit and dog-patrolled) between the two forms. Some people thought that Kapuściński made things up, that (for example) the marvellous recollections by the Ethiopian courtiers in *The Emperor* were largely imaginative reconstruction or even fiction. There may be something in that. Kapuściński, I think, did what many journalists do at times: he selected from his notes, perhaps changed the order in which things were said, dropped the parts which didn't interest him, and then sharpened up the best passages – not for 'sensational revelation' purposes, but for literary effect. For me, such 'heightening' doesn't really detract from what was written, as long as the text is not presented as a verbatim record.

But not many of his readers have absorbed Kapuściński as a thinker, as an intellectual who enjoyed philosophical theorising and ethical reflection on the margins of Catholic theology. He was always a wide, compulsive reader, but this interest in abstract ethics did not show clearly in his work until *Travels With Herodotus*, the last of his major books to be translated into English.[3] *The Other* will therefore come as a surprise. It consists of a group of collected lectures, one dating back to 1990, but the others delivered in the last five years of his life at gatherings in Vienna and in Kraków. Their subject is the encounter, above all the white European encounter, ~ with unfamiliar cultures whose difference may be distilled into an essential Otherness and loaded with every kind of discourse of ethical and technical superiority. Kapuściński saw a lot of that distilling. Himself immune to its products (his view was the Herodotean assessment: that all peoples are different and that it's natural that each ¯ people thinks its own ways are best), he has witnessed every variety of imperial arrogance and ignorance. ~

Otherness is not, of course, a new topic. It's interesting that Kapuściński's references and inspirations on the subject are almost all from Polish sources. Malinowski is one. Another is Father Józef Tischner, a senior Kraków theologian and a widely read writer on ethics who was very close to the late Pope John Paul II. Tischner, in turn, drew strongly on the work and thought of Emmanuel Lévinas (d. 1995), and his insistence on the

3. R. Kapuściński, *Travels with Herodotus*, trans. K. Glowczewska, London: Knopf, 2007.

primacy of ethics in philosophical enquiry. Lévinas (only survivor of a Jewish family in Lithuania which perished in the Holocaust) had moved to Paris in 1923, and studied later in Freiburg under Husserl and Heidegger. Although he was not Polish and remained loyal to Judaism, Lévinas's thought deeply influenced Polish Catholic intellectuals – including Karol Wojtyła, the future Pope – during the Communist period.

'The Other' was his central topic. Lévinas considered that philosophers were wasting their time on metaphysics and epistemology. Although he lived in France, the land of Descartes, he did not believe that 'I think, therefore I am', but that 'the self is only possible through the recognition of the Other' (a famous phrase quoted in these lectures).

This notion informs the conclusions Kapuściński draws from his travelling and reporting encounters in other continents. But there is a background here which the reader needs to bear in mind. This author spent most of his life writing for a Polish readership, a readership isolated by the Cold War inside its own frontiers, which had inherited a traditional taste for Otherness as a form of exotic entertainment. Throughout central Europe, and to some extent in Germany too, landlocked peoples without overseas empires or the opportunity for distant travel longed for amazing tales about remote continents. In the nineteenth and twentieth centuries, a whole genre of travel writing sprang up to satisfy that longing for palm trees, wide-open spaces, strange animals and bizarre tribes. The German novels of Karl May, set in an imaginary Wild West, gripped many landlocked imaginations. Later, gifted journalists set out as world-travelling reporters, serving their Czech or Polish or Hungarian readers a diet of thrilling and addictive articles which described the Other not only in terms of landscape and exotic customs, but as sites of inhuman exploitation, hunger and suffering. In the first half of the century, it was the dazzling Egon Erwin Kisch from Prague, the *rasende Reporter* (globe-trotting newsman) of his times, who helped to convert the mood of this Other-writing from uncritical awe to an anti-imperial exposé journalism with a distinctly socialist content.

Kapuściński quite clearly emerges from this tradition as one of its last exponents. When he began to write journalism, over fifty years ago, Poland had been effectively cut off from the world since 1939 – first by Nazi occupation, and then by a Soviet-modelled Communist regime. The hunger for news and images from 'out there' was desperate. The 'out there' Poles really wanted to hear from was of course Western Europe, but reports from those parts were tightly censored. Next best, but still delicious for starved readers, was reporting from the big world of Africa, Latin America and Asia, and that is what Ryszard Kapuściński was able to provide. And the censors were relatively relaxed about those continents; to describe suffering, capitalist greed and exploitation in the Congo or Guatemala was, after all, no more than to describe reality. Kapuściński flourished, doing an agency reporter's grind for much of the time, but also contributing reflective and descriptive features and magazine articles which made him famous and popular in his own country.

As he grew older, he began to reflect more – as journalists often do – on the perspective he had acquired. Western journalists usually know more about psychotherapy than about Christian philosophy or phenomenology; they wrestle with guilt-making problems about voyeurism, repressed attraction to violence, the dishonesty of claims to reproduce the experience of battle. But Kapuściński, as this book shows, is less interested in himself than in the way in which Otherness is manufactured, experienced and understood in the world. He writes in a vein which is already slightly old-fashioned, a voice very much from the later twentieth century. His generation did not – and does not – wish to turn away from the experience of two world wars, from the crimes of two unimaginably murderous totalitarian systems, and from the 'modernist' notion of 'mass society'.

— He relates, in these pages, 'the transformations and crisis of Western civilisation, and in particular the crisis and atrophy of interpersonal relations between the Self and the Other' to the sort of collectivist triumphalism encouraged by dictators. But Kapuściński is the last person to see the remedy in an atomising individualism. In line with his gurus, Tischner and Lévinas, he believes that 'genuine' individualism – the recognition of selfhood – can only be brought about by contact with and recognition of the Other, the being who is external to oneself and yet a reflection of oneself. As Tischner put it, in his very post-Cartesian way, 'I know that I am, because I know that *another* is'. It is an ethical approach which became widespread in modern Christianity during the postwar decades. Some forty years ago, when I was living in Berlin, I was struck by the language of an Evangelical Church poster addressed to *Du und der Du neben Dir* – 'You, and the You next to You'.

It could be said that, in concentrating only on negative Otherness as perceived by white Europeans venturing into other continents, Kapuściński is limiting his subject. The perception of Otherness, leading to the treatment of the Other as less than human, has been an intra-European habit for many millennia, even though it has only just been given a title. It is needless to recall how settled peoples in Europe treated nomadic peoples, or how 'indigenous' populations from time to time tried to exterminate urban minorities (Jews, Lombards, Armenians, Flemings, to name a few) as alien and unnatural beings. But Kapuściński, it must be said, had a cunning habit of writing about distant lands in ways which instantly suggested domestic comparisons to his readers. It was a classic way of evading the censors (another was the 'historical' novel which was really about the present). For instance, his uncompleted trilogy about autocrats who thought that 'development' could make democracy unnecessary (Haile Selassie, the last Shah of Persia, and Idi Amin of Uganda) unmistakeably lampooned the rule of Edward Gierek, leader of Communist Poland in the 1970s. He never wrote a book about the racial and national prejudices that were endemic in Poland. All the same, his awareness of shocking events in his own country gave his reporting of communal hatreds and fear in Africa a special edge.

When he does write about Europe in this book, it is with hope. The colonial empires have gone, the Cold War is over, and it is possible to replace mass society with global society. The world is merging and becoming multicultural, and Otherness is becoming not just a negative reaction between white Europeans and those they have dominated, but a positive encounter between liberated peoples on every continent. As Kapuściński remarks in these pages, Europe is now free to rediscover its old Enlightenment principles from the era

— when European thought tried to build bridges of understanding with Others. Referring to these efforts, and carrying on with them, is not just an ethical duty but also an urgent task for our time in a world where everything is so fragile and where there is so much demagogy, disorientation, fanaticism and bad will.

Neal Ascherson
July 2008

THE VIENNESE LECTURES

I

Conquest and Exchange

The terms 'Other' or 'Others' can be understood in all sorts of ways and used in various meanings and contexts, to distinguish gender, for example, or generation, or nationality, or religion and so on. In my case I use these terms mainly to distinguish Europeans, people from the West, whites, from those whom I call 'Others' – that is, non-Europeans, or non-whites, while fully aware that for the latter, the former are just as much 'Others'.

The genre I do my best to pursue is literary reportage based on my experiences of many years spent travelling around the world. Each piece of reportage has many authors, and it is only thanks to long-established custom that we sign the text with a single name. In fact it may well be the most collective, co-written literary genre of all, because dozens of people contribute to producing it – the people we meet and talk to on the world's roads, who tell us stories about their lives, the life of their community, events they have taken part in or heard about from others. These foreign people, whom we often do not know well, are not only among our richest sources of knowledge about the world, but also help us to do our jobs in many other ways – they arrange contacts, lend us their homes, or quite simply save our lives.

Each of these people, whom we meet along the road and across the world, is in a way twofold; each one consists of two beings whom it is often difficult to separate, a fact that we do not always realise. One of these beings is a person like the rest of us: he has his joys and sorrows, his good and bad days; he is glad of his successes, does not like to be hungry and does not like it when he is cold; he feels pain as suffering and misery, and good fortune as satisfying and fulfilling. The other being, who overlaps and is interwoven with the first, is a person as bearer of racial features, and as bearer of culture, beliefs and convictions. Neither of these beings appears in a pure, isolated state – they coexist, having a reciprocal effect on each other.

However, the problem – and here lies the difficulty of my profession as a reporter – is that this relationship existing within each of us, between the person as individual and personality and the person as bearer of culture and race, is not immobile, rigid or static, not fixed inside him for good. On the contrary, its typical features are dynamism, mobility, variability and differences in intensity, depending on the external context, the demands of the current moment, the expectations of the environment or even one's own mood and stage of life. As a result we never know whom we are going to meet, even though by name and appearance it may be someone who is already familiar to us. And what about when we come into contact with a person we are seeing for the first time? So every encounter with the Other is an enigma, an unknown quantity – I would even say a mystery.

Before it comes to this encounter, however, we reporters are already somehow prepared in advance, usually through reading (in the years when television did not yet exist). In fact, the whole of world literature is devoted to Others, from the Upanishads through the I Ching and Chuang Tzu, from Homer and Hesiod through Gilgamesh and the Old Testament, from the Popol Vuh to the Torah and the Koran. And what about the great medieval travellers who set off for the far ends of the planet to see Others, from Giovanni da Pian del Carpine to Ibn Battuta, from Marco Polo to Ibn Khaldun and Kiu Chang-chun? In some young minds this reading matter ignited a desire to reach the most far-flung corners of the world, in order to meet and get to know Others. It was the typical illusion of space – the belief that whatever is far away is different, and the farther away it is, the more different it is.

'In some minds', I said, because despite the general view an obsession with travel is not a commonly found passion. Man is by nature a settled creature, a trait that has been fixed in him ever since agriculture and the art of building cities were devised. Man usually only leaves his nest under duress – driven out by war or famine, by plague, drought or fire. Sometimes he sets off because he is being persecuted for his beliefs, and sometimes in search of work or opportunities for his children. But for many people the world outside is a source of anxiety, arousing fear of the unexpected, or even the terror of death. Every culture has a whole set of charms and magic spells designed to protect anyone setting off on the road, who is bid farewell amid outbursts of weeping and regret as if he were about to climb the scaffold.

When I say travel, naturally I do not mean tourist trips. In a reporter's understanding, a journey is a challenge and an effort, involving hard work and dedication; it is a difficult task, an ambitious project to accomplish. As we travel, we can feel that something important is happening, that we are taking part in something of which we are at once both witnesses and creators, that there is a duty incumbent upon us, and that we are responsible for something.

And in fact we are responsible for the road we are travelling. We often feel sure that we are walking or driving down a particular road just this once in our lives, and that we shall never return to it again, so we must not miss anything from this journey, we cannot overlook or lose anything, because we are going to give an account of it all, write a report, a story – we are going to examine our conscience. And so, as we travel we concentrate, we focus our attention and sharpen our hearing. The road we are on is very important, because each step along it takes us nearer to an encounter with the Other, and that is exactly why we are there. Would we otherwise voluntarily expose ourselves to hardships and take on the risk of all sorts of discomfort and danger?

It is not only that voluntary travel, travel as a way of life, is a rarity – deep curiosity about the world is not a common phenomenon either. Most people have little interest in it. History tells of entire civilisations that demonstrated no interest at all in the world beyond. Africa never built a single ship to sail away and see what lies beyond the seas surrounding it. Its people never even tried to reach neighbouring Europe. Chinese civilisation was even more insular: it simply fenced itself off from the rest of the world with a huge wall. (In fact, empires on horseback, such as the Persians, Arabs and Mongols, behaved differently, but their aim was not to get to know

the world – instead it was armed conquest and enslavement. Moreover, these empires only enjoyed relatively
short periods of ascendancy and oppression, and then
collapsed to be buried in sand forever.)

In this march of civilisations, Europe will be the
exception, because it is the only one, right from its
Greek beginnings, to show *curiosity about the world* and a
desire not just to conquer and dominate it, but also to
have *knowledge* of it; and in the case of its best minds,
nothing but knowledge, understanding and closer relations with a view to forming a human community. In
their full clarity, complexity and drama our relations with
the rest of the inhabitants of the planet – with Others –
will be a constant theme here.

These relations have a long history. In literature they
start with the great *History* of Herodotus. The Greek
historian, who lived and wrote 2,500 years ago, shows us
that already in those days the world was populated by a
large number of fully formed, mature societies with well-
developed cultures and a strong sense of their own
identities; in short, that the first European, in other
words the Greek – although he called anyone non-Greek
barbaros, a speaker of incomprehensible gibberish – was
aware that the Other was in fact *someone*. Herodotus
himself wrote about Others without contempt or hatred,
he tried to get to know and understand them, and often

directly demonstrated the many ways in which they were superior to the Greeks.

Herodotus was aware of man's sedentary nature and realised that to get to know Others you must set off on a journey, go to them, and show a desire to meet them; so he kept travelling, visiting the Egyptians and the Scythians, the Persians and the Lydians, remembering everything he heard from them, as well as what he saw for himself. In short, he wanted to know them because he understood that to know ourselves we have to know Others, who act as the mirror in which we see ourselves reflected; he knew that to understand ourselves better we have to understand Others, to compare ourselves with them, to measure ourselves against them. As a citizen of the world, he did not believe that we should isolate ourselves from Others, or slam the gates in their faces. Xenophobia, Herodotus implied, is a sickness of people who are scared, suffering an inferiority complex, terrified by the prospect of seeing themselves in the mirror of the culture of Others. And his entire book is a solid construction of mirrors in which we keep getting a better and clearer view of, above all, Greece and the Greeks.

Later, however, encounters between Europeans and non-Europeans often assumed an extremely violent and bloody character. In fact, it had happened before Herodotus, when Greece clashed with Persia, and after him too, during the conquests of Alexander the Great, the expansion of the Roman Empire, the Crusades, the Spanish Conquest and so on.

Incidentally, let us note that we think in such a Eurocentric way – as do most of the historians known to us – that whenever we talk or write about our relation to Others, for example about conflict with Others, we mean conflict between Europeans and non-Europeans; yet confrontations and wars of this kind have claimed a sea of victims within the non-European world, where the Mongols waged wars against the Chinese, the Aztecs against neighbouring tribes, Muslims against Hindus, and so on.

In short, the clash of civilisations is not a modern invention, but has been happening throughout the history of mankind. Besides, we should remember that conflict, collision, is just one quite unnecessary form of contact between civilisations. Another one that features even more often is exchange, which sometimes happens at the same time as conflict, as if the two processes were linked. Here is an example. In the early 1990s I was in Liberia, where there was civil war, and I went to the front with a unit of government troops. The front ran along a river, whose banks were joined at that spot by a bridge. Next to the bridge, on the government side there was a large market. On the other side of the river, occupied by Charles Taylor's rebels, there was nothing, just empty fields. On this front along the river, the mortars roared away and the shooting went on until midday. But in the afternoon peace reigned, and the rebels came over the bridge to go shopping at the market. On the way they handed their weapons over to a government patrol, which gave them back when they returned to their side with the goods they had bought at the market. And so in a place of armed, bloody conflict there was simultaneously the exchange of produce and other goods. It is the situation, the circumstances, the context, that decide whether we see a person as enemy or as partner at any given moment. The Other can be both of these, and that is the basis of his changeable, elusive nature, his contradictory behaviour, whose motives he himself is sometimes incapable of understanding.

At the end of the European Middle Ages and at the start of modern times, Europe's great expedition to conquer the world, enslave the Other and pillage his possessions wrote pages of blood and cruelty into the history of our planet. The scale of genocidal practices in that era, which lasted for more than three centuries, would not be surpassed until the twentieth century, when it would take the macabre form of the Holocaust.

The image of the Other that Europeans had when they set out to conquer the planet is of a naked savage, a cannibal and pagan, whose humiliation and oppression is the sacred right and duty of the European – who is white and Christian. The cause of the exceptional brutality and cruelty that typified whites was not only the lust for gold and slaves that consumed their minds and blinded the ruling elites of Europe, but also the incredibly low standard of culture and morals among those sent out as the vanguard for contact with Others. In those days ships' crews consisted largely of villains, criminals and bandits, the inveterate, avowed rabble; at best they were tramps, homeless people and failures, the reason being that it was hard to persuade a normal person to choose to go on a voyage of adventure that often ended in death.

The fact that for centuries Europe has been sending out its worst, most repulsive representatives to meet Others, and to meet them for the first time into the bargain, is bound to cast a sad shadow over our relations with Others, to shape our common views about them, and to fix stereotypes, prejudices and phobias in our minds that sometimes still appear in one form or another to this day. I am sure of this even to this day, when I hear apparently serious people say, for instance, that the only solution for Africa is to colonise it again.

Conquer, colonise, master, make dependent – this reaction to Others recurs constantly throughout the history of the world. The idea of equality with the Other only occurs to the human mind very late on, many thousands of years after man first left traces of his presence on Earth.

In talking of Others and relations with Others, I am limiting myself here to intercultural and interracial relationships, because this is the sphere with which I have had most contact. If we look at it historically we can see how, after three centuries of brutal and relentless expansion by the European courts and European capital (and we are talking not just about the conquest of overseas populations and territories but about overland operations too, such as the destruction of the Siberian races by the Russians), in the eighteenth century there begins a gradual, admittedly partial, yet important change in atmosphere and attitude to the Other, to Others, who are usually non-European societies. It is the age of Enlightenment and humanism, and of the revolutionary discovery that the non-white, non-Christian savage, that monstrous Other so unlike us *is a human being too*.

The road to this revelation was opened, above all, by literature. Works appeared by Daniel Defoe and Jonathan Swift, Jean-Jacques Rousseau and Voltaire, Fontenelle and Montesquieu, Goethe and Herder. It was an extraordinary, dazzling eruption of talents, hearts and minds; dozens of authors reviled the abuses and cruelty perpetrated by conquistadors of all descriptions and various nations, crying that those Others, whom they have robbed and murdered, are our equals, 'our brothers in Christ', deserving respect and esteem. The antislavery movement developed, cartography flourished, and scientific expeditions were organised, not so much to conquer and enslave but rather to discover new lands and become familiar with other, previously unknown peoples and their cultures. Instead of fear of Others, there was more and more curiosity about them, and a desire to get to know them better. This came with an incredible development in reportage and all sorts of other travel literature including, to mention just a few of the now classic works, the writing of James Cook and Mungo Park, Richard Pococke's *A Description of the East* and, above all, the Abbé Prévost's *Histoire générale des voyages*, a collection of tales from around the world. As his contemporary, the great Swiss traveller, scientist and philosopher Albrecht von Haller, would write in the mid-eighteenth century:

Nothing is better able to dispel prejudices than familiarity with many peoples of disparate customs, laws and opinions – an otherness that for the price of a minor effort teaches us to cast off what makes people different, and to regard as the voice of nature the things on which all peoples agree: because the first laws of nature are the same for all peoples . . . Not to offend anyone, to grant each man his due.[4]

At the time, Haller's views divided many thinkers, writers and travellers, who to a large extent set the tone of the contemporary epoch, sometimes defined as the age of humanitarianism and sentimentalism. They included the great French historian and philosopher Guillaume Raynal, an *Encyclopédiste* who reviled slavery and colonial exploitation with fervent passion. It was the first time the profile of the Other as a being, unique and unrepeatable, had been drawn with such clarity and humanity. This was a great step in the transition from the clichéd image of the unpredictable savage to the distinctive figure who represents another culture or race. It represented a complete revolution in European thinking, initiating a transition from the image of the vile barbarian to someone with human features who belongs to the family of man.

For the first time on this scale and with such intensity the Other became an internal problem for European culture, an ethnic problem for all of us.

4. A. von Haller, *Sammlung kleiner hallerischen Schriften*, trans. Antonia Lloyd-Jones, Bern: Haller, 1772, p. 136.

II

The Meaning of Difference

Relations between Europeans and Others can be divided, in extremely reduced and simplified terms, into several eras:

1. The era of merchants and envoys, when people on the road came into contact with Others, either on trade routes or when sent by one of the potentates of the time on a diplomatic mission to another country. This period lasted roughly until the fifteenth century.
2. The era of great geographical discoveries. (Third World patriots bridle at this term. What do you mean, they say, America was discovered, or Asia? We knew about those continents from the dawn of time. We have always lived there!) This is a period of conquest,

slaughter and plunder, the real dark ages in relations between Europeans and Others. It lasted for several hundred years.

3. The era of Enlightenment and humanism, openness to Others, the first attempts at understanding them, making human contacts, and developing the exchange not only of goods but also of cultural and spiritual values.

4. The Enlightenment gave rise to a new era that continues to this day, and which can be characterised by three successive turning points:
   a) the turning point of anthropologists;
   b) the turning point of Lévinas;[5]
   c) the turning point of multiculturalism.

The era of greatest significance for our considerations is the Age of Enlightenment. In relations between Europeans and Others it closed a period of 'wildness' and opened the modern era. A new language, a new vocabulary appeared. The *Encyclopédistes* promoted the idea of

5. Emmanuel Lévinas (1906–95) was a French philosopher, religious thinker and Talmudic commentator. He was born in Kovno, Russia (now Kaunas, Lithuania), but in 1923 went to study at Strasbourg University, and then Freiburg, where he studied under Husserl and Heidegger. His ideas on ethical responsibility for 'the Other' influenced several generations of French philosophers and both Jewish and Christian theologians, including Pope John Paul II. His major work, *Totality and Infinity*, was published in 1961.

universal learning, Goethe dreamed of the emergence of a world literature, and concepts such as 'world government' or the 'citizen of the world' appeared. Even though the word 'savage' was still in use, it was supplemented with the adjective 'noble' – 'the noble savage'.

Of course the slave trade and colonial expansion were still going on, but something in the thinking and morality of Europeans had started to change, and it had become necessary to consider appearances – people no longer spoke of 'colonialism', but of 'the mission to civilise', 'conversion' or 'bringing help to poor, backward people'.

In this era of cultural change, passing from narrow Eurocentrism to more universal visions that embrace the entire world, a new branch of social science was born – anthropology. Anthropology is aimed towards the Other, dedicated exclusively to him. Contained within it is the idea of understanding the Other by getting to know him, the idea of accepting diversity and otherness as constituent features of mankind.

With time, two schools arose and developed among the anthropologists: evolutionists and diffusionists. In fact, in a different shape and form, and also under various names, such a division exists to this day, occasionally making itself apparent when new arguments arise between the two schools. The evolutionists believe in the inevitable progress of all mankind; they maintain that all human societies develop from the lowest, 'primitive' ones to the highest, civilised ones, and thus that all people in the world follow the same common path of development and progress; that it is just a matter of time before those who are last catch up with those who are farthest in front. Just as importantly, the evolutionists believe in the psychological unity of mankind, and as proof they offer the cultural similarities that they have discovered and identified in various societies around the world. In short, the evolutionists are optimists, who believe in the cohesion and unity of the family of man; they are citizens of the world and regard all kinds of Others as such too – as we would put it nowadays, they are globalists.

In contrast, the diffusionists reckon many different civilisations and cultures have existed and continue to exist on our planet. Depending on the place and time, these come into contact with each other and a process of fusion, combination and borrowing is formed between them; there is constant, dynamic communication, a creative dialogue, a lively, compound exchange. The diversity and multiplicity of cultures, and the hybridity produced by intercultural contact – that is what fascinates the diffusionists. They perceive Others not as a homogeneous, identical society, but as a diverse, multi-coloured, multilingual throng whose individual groups live separately, have their own gods and walk their own paths.

If the evolutionists are globalists, as I have mentioned, the diffusionists are anti-globalists; not in the sense of fighting globalisation, but because to their minds the world is like a Persian carpet, intricate and extremely rich in its diversity.

Although representatives of the two schools have argued and still do, their intentions are in every respect sincere and inspiring – their main concern is how best to get to know and understand Others, describe them and give us a closer view of them.

In their aim to know Others as well as possible, in a perfectly pure state, so to speak, unsullied by alien influences, some of the anthropologists (later called functionalists) set off to the remotest places on the planet, usually tiny islands in the Pacific or inaccessible regions of Africa, to investigate and record how the society of Others operated in its natural cultural environment. This resulted in a series of works, often of excellent literary and scholarly value, which open European eyes to the multiplicity, wealth, logical and functional cohesion of cultures previously unknown to them. Such authors as Rivers, Radcliffe-Brown or Evans-Pritchard proved that the cultures of Others were just as valuable and reasonable as European culture, except that they were simply *other*.

A step further – but what an important step! – was taken by Malinowski, who made so-called fieldwork an indispensable condition of getting to know Others: it is not just necessary to go to them, but also to live among them or with them.[6] So he set off for one of the islands in the Trobriand Archipelago, and there, in the middle of a village, he pitched his tent. Malinowski discovered to his amazement that the white people who had been living on these islands for decades not only lived far away from the local villages, but what they said about the native population was a load of nonsense, nothing but false, absurd stereotypes. In short, the white man in the tropics is the worst, least reliable source of information about local peoples and cultures.

The former shuns the latter, because an encounter with Others is not a simple, automatic thing, but involves will and an effort that not everyone is always ready to undertake. Fieldwork is not only recommended for anthropologists, but is also a fundamental condition for the job of a reporter. In this sense we can regard

6. The Polish-born anthropologist Bronisław Malinowski (1884–1942) was a pioneer of ethnographic fieldwork and of reciprocity, conducting major studies of Melanesia. He lived among the natives in the Trobriand Islands, where he was stranded throughout the First World War. Living on such intimate terms with the local people led to his theories of participant observation, which are now key to anthropological methodology. In 1922 he sealed his reputation with the publication of *Argonauts of the Western Pacific*.

Malinowski as the creator of anthropological reportage, which developed everywhere from then on.

The texts produced as a result of fieldwork had a strong influence on European thinking about Others, because they proved that these Others were not hordes of inscrutable, idle primitives, but that they lived within highly developed cultures which had complex, sophisticated structures and hierarchies. In relations with Others, in our attitude to them, we rose another rung up the ladder.

Although fieldwork played such an important, positive role in expanding our knowledge about the human family, it had two weak points, which in time brought it to an impasse.

Firstly, each of the anthropologists studied and attempted to describe one single, usually small tribe, while in Africa for instance there were several thousand tribes at the time (the turn of the nineteenth and twentieth centuries). Additionally, it soon turned out that most of these societies had their own distinct structures, traditions and even languages, and that research conducted on one tribe did not provide the key to describing a second, so individual, separate observations did not add up into a cohesive, comprehensive picture. Separate pieces existed that could not be arranged into an intelligible mosaic.

Secondly, an effort was made to research and get to know traditional cultures as if they occurred in a pure form, in which they had existed for centuries in isolation and seclusion. So they were described as static structures, immobile and fixed for good and all, while in reality they were undergoing constant change; especially in our times, a continual, often thorough transformation. Before Evans-Pritchard, for example, had managed to describe the Zande tribe, it already looked completely different or had entirely dispersed and ceased to exist, along with its culture and its gods. At this point a period of accelerated, increased migration had set in, when millions and millions of people moved to the cities, and that mainstay of tradition, the village, was depopulated as its people were decimated by famine, civil war, drought and epidemics. The person we meet and get to know in the big cities of the Third World is already another Other – the product of an urban, hybrid culture that is hard to define, the descendant of various contradictory worlds, a composite creature of fluid, impermanent contours and features. Nowadays it is exactly this kind of Other that we are usually dealing with.

Now I shall talk about the turning point brought about by the philosophy of Emmanuel Lévinas. I regard this philosophy as a reaction, among other things, to mankind's experiences in the first half of the twentieth century, especially to the transformations and crises of

Western civilisation, and in particular the crisis and atrophy of interpersonal relations between the Self and the Other. The problem of the Other, of our attitude to him, is one of the main themes of Lévinas's reflections. The meaning of, and need for, Lévinas's approach are of the utmost importance.

At the outbreak of the First World War, Lévinas was eight years old, and when the Second World War erupted he was thirty-three. Thus he was growing up in the years when mass society was forming in Europe and the two totalitarian systems, communism and fascism, were coming into existence. The person living in a mass society was typified by anonymity, lack of social ties, indifference towards the Other and, as a result of losing his cultural identity, defencelessness and susceptibility to evil, with all its tragic results; the most inhuman symbol of this phenomenon would be the Holocaust.

It is this indifference towards the Other, which creates an atmosphere capable in particular circumstances of leading to Auschwitz, that Lévinas countered with his philosophy. Stop, he seems to be saying to the man hurrying along in the rushing crowd. There beside you is another person. Meet him. This sort of encounter is the greatest event, the most vital experience of all. Look at the Other's face as he offers it to you. Through this face he shows you yourself: more than that – he brings you closer to God.

Lévinas goes further. He says you must not only meet the Other, accept him and converse with him, but you must also take responsibility for him. Lévinas's philosophy distinguishes the individual and singles it out. He indicates that apart from myself there is also someone Other, but – if I fail to make the effort to notice or to show a desire to meet – we shall pass each other by indifferently, coldly and without feeling, blandly and heartlessly. Meanwhile, says Lévinas, the Other has a face, and it is a sacred book in which good is recorded.

Here our interest is in Lévinas's thesis about the fundamental meaning of difference – that we accept the Other, although he is different, and that this difference, this otherness is rich and valuable, it is a good thing. Yet at the same time this difference does not erase my identification with the Other: 'I am someone Other.'

If the Enlightenment told us that the Other is a person equal to us, a member of the same family to which we belong, and if compared with the Enlightenment later anthropology took a step forwards, showing the European that the person from another race and tradition has his own, highly developed social and spiritual culture – then Emmanuel Lévinas took us further still, proclaiming praise for and the superiority of the Other, and our duty to take responsibility for him. Lévinas even went so far as to say the Other is our master and that he is closer to God than I am, and that our relation with the Other should be a movement towards Good. Here we are dealing with postulating philosophy, deeply ethical, demanding dedication and heroism, that can only be realised somewhere beyond the horizon of the average person's everyday experiences. A philosophy whose chief imperative is the commandment 'Do not kill!'

In reading Lévinas's works two points stand out. Firstly, in the thoughts expressed in *Le temps et l'autre* the Other is always an individual, a single person. However, man when he is alone is usually more 'human' than when he is a member of a crowd, an excited mass. Individually we are wiser and better, less inscrutable. Becoming part of a group can change the same quiet, friendly individual into a devil.

Secondly, Lévinas talked about an Other who is of the same white race and inhabits the same Western cultural circle. He did not talk about situations where a white person encounters an Other who has a different skin colour, believes in different gods and speaks in a language he cannot understand. What then? I put this question to a great expert on Lévinas's philosophy, Professor Barbara Skarga. She replied,

> But his philosophy is a framework that you have to fill in with your own experience and observations.

Lévinas never stops seeking ways to reach the Other, he wants to free us from the restraints of selfishness, from indifference, keep us from the temptation to be separate, to isolate ourselves and be withdrawn. He shows us a new dimension of the Self, namely that it is not just a solitary individual, but that the composition of that Self also includes the Other, and like this a new kind of person or being is created.

III

The Challenge of Multiculturalism

The next great breakthrough in our relations between ourselves and Others began in the final decade of the twentieth century. This was the start of the current era of the multicultural world. As we entered it, we were already equipped with a wealth of experience:

- the experience of the Renaissance, which had opened the European mind to the presence of Others – people from continents, races and religions beyond Europe;
- the experience brought by anthropological investigations that had provided us with knowledge of other societies and cultures, their great diversity, great complexity and noble values;
- finally, the philosophy of Lévinas, which focused our attention on the Other as an individual, a

personality (anthropology by contrast researched and described communities), as a unique person whom we should not just notice but also include in our experience and for whom we should take responsibility.

So we have arrived in a new era, a new situation. What caused it to arise? What does it consist of? At this point any answer can only be an attempt at an answer, because we are talking about the present time, in which everything is changing, and at a rate that hinders any meaningful, deeper reflection. This new era, which we could also define as a time of transition from mass to global society, has arisen at a moment when two phenomena are coinciding: on the one hand the electronic communications revolution is undergoing acceleration and globalisation, and on the other the Cold War order is collapsing.

Thanks to this our planet is becoming an open, or potentially open, space. I think this will determine the future fate of mankind, at least over the next few decades. Above all, it puts our relations with Others in a new situation. For five centuries Europe dominated the world, not just politically and economically, but also culturally. It imposed its faith and established the law, the scale of values, models of behaviour and languages. Our relations with Others were always asymmetrical, and for our part were invariably imperious, overbearing and paternalistic. The long, 500-year existence of such an uneven, unfair system has produced numerous ingrained habits among its participants.

However, in the mid-twentieth century the process of decolonisation began, and two-thirds of the world's population acquired, at least nominally, the status of free citizens. Now they returned to their roots and revived their cultures. They started to emphasise the significance of these cultures with pride, and to gain strength from them. Still locked up and ossified in its Eurocentrism, Europe did not seem to notice, or preferred not to notice, that on our planet various non-European civilisations were gaining in importance, dynamism and life, and were more and more firmly and clearly demanding a place at the world's table. It was a time of great challenge for Europe, which had to find itself a new place at this table; never again would it sit there on an exclusive principle, unthreatened and autocratic.

At this same moment the Cold War was ending, the division of the planet into opposing blocs was ending, and a new world was taking shape, more mobile and open than ever before.

Two factors were especially conducive to all this mobility and freedom. The first was the rebirth of the spirit of democracy, which started at the close of the past century. The era of military coups and military regimes was ending, and so was the era of dictators, one-party systems, economic autarky, censorship and borders fenced with barbed wire. Democracy was becoming fashionable, no one objected to it, and even the most undemocratic parties had the adjective 'democratic' in their names.

This pro-democracy atmosphere has been enormously conducive to human mobility. The world is in motion on an unprecedented scale. People of the most varied races and cultures are meeting each other all over this more and more populated planet. If formerly, traditionally, in saying 'Others' we simply meant non-Europeans, now these relations are as extensive and varied as they can be, on a never-ending scale of possibilities covering all races and cultures – for the Chinese the Others will be Malaysians and Indians, for the Arabs they will be Latin Americans and Congolese – the number of combinations is huge. A new Other has been born: a non-European who is Other in relation to another non-European. On my travels about the world in the last few years I have noticed increasingly often and ever more clearly how relations, connections and an exchange are developing between people from Africa and Asia for example, or the Pacific islands and the Caribbean, who have never been to

Europe, do not know much about it and are not even interested in it.

This global migration fever so typical of the present day involves many factors; let us mention just two of them. Firstly, the ongoing electronic revolution and the vast development of communications that comes with it – transport, telecommunications and so on. From slow sea routes mankind switches to air routes, greatly reducing travelling time, increasing a person's mobility and widening his contacts with Others. Secondly, the deepening inequalities in the world, and above all the rising awareness of those inequalities. In our era the poorer people are trying to reduce their numbers and eliminate these differences, not by way of confrontation but by permeation, migrating to richer regions and countries.

In such a reality the number of interpersonal encounters and contacts increases sharply, and it is their nature and quality, and our increasingly frequent and various relations with Others, that will determine the climate of the world we live in. As in every sphere of life, so too in this one everything starts to take on the structure of a net – changeable and dynamic, lacking any fixed points of reference. More and more people within it have problems defining their own identity, or determining their own social or cultural affiliation. They feel lost, and are increasingly susceptible to the suggestions of nationalists and racists, who tell them to regard the Other as a threat, an enemy, the cause of all their tiresome frustrations and fears.

The dialogue with Others has never been and will never be easy, especially today, when everything is on such an enormous scale and is so complicated that it is hard to take in and control, and when many forces are working to obstruct this dialogue, or even to make it impossible. But even without these short-term political, ideological or economically motivated interests and aims there are other, substantial, fundamental problems.

One of them is the focus of the Sapir–Whorf hypothesis of so-called linguistic relativity. In the simplest terms, it says that thinking is formed on the basis of language, and as we speak in different languages, each of us creates his own image of the world, unlike any other. These images are not compatible and are not replaceable. For this reason dialogue, though not impossible, demands a serious effort, patience, and the will of its participants to understand and communicate. Being aware of the fact that in conversing with the Other I am communing with someone who at the same time sees the world differently from me and understands it another way is important in creating a positive atmosphere for dialogue.

The next problem in contacts between us and them, the Others, is that all civilisations have a tendency towards narcissism, and the stronger the civilisation, the more clearly this tendency will appear. It spurs civilisations into conflict with others, triggering their arrogance and lust for domination. This always involves contempt for Others. In old China this arrogance took on a very subtle form – it was expressed through pity for anyone who was not born Chinese. This narcissism was and is masked by all manner of rhetoric – usually to do with being the chosen race, or having been summoned to a salvation mission, or both combined.

The next problem is the ambivalent nature of our first reaction to Others. On the one hand, one person needs another; he seeks him out and knows he cannot live without Others. At the same time, at the first moment of contact the initial reaction will be mistrust, uncertainty and fear. And all these feelings and states resist any efforts to control them or overcome them.

Meanwhile culture, not to say man himself too, is formed through contact with Others (which is why everything so heavily depends on the quality of this contact). For Simmel, the human individual is shaped in the process, in relations, in connection with Others. Sapir says the same thing: 'The real place where culture happens is in personal interactions.' Others, let us repeat, are the mirror in which I look at myself, and which tells me who I am. When I lived in my country I was not aware that I am a white man and that this could have any significance for my fate. Only once I found myself in Africa was I immediately informed of this by the sight of its black inhabitants. Thanks to them I discovered my own skin colour, which I never would have thought about alone. Others cast a new light on my own history for me. When they hear about the Nazi concentration camps and the Soviet Gulag, they are amazed that the white man is so cruel to other white men. Why do white people hate each other so much that they murder by the million? In their eyes, in the twentieth century the white race committed suicide. That emboldened them to start the struggle against colonialism.

There are many other difficulties, question marks and even mysteries on the road to our encounter with Others. Yet this encounter and coexistence on our globalising planet is inevitable, because we live in a multicultural world. Not because there are more of these cultures now than ever before – in fact their number is declining. Writing 2,500 years ago, Herodotus mentions hundreds of tribes, creeds and languages he had come across in person or heard about, and he enumerates them as something obvious, existing for him since time immemorial. Later, in the centuries that follow, dozens of other travellers and merchants were consistently amazed by the rich panorama of peoples and cultures that they happened to meet during their expeditions.

What is new today is that awareness has grown of the presence and importance of these cultures: awareness of their multiplicity, of their right to exist and to own a separate identity. And this has coincided with the great revolution in communications, which has enabled these cultures to have multiple encounters, a polyphonic, many-sided dialogue, and also, in various situations, argument and conflict. All this happens in a world that is more democratised than ever before, which enables Others to speak out and say their bit, though admittedly not everyone is willing to listen.

The act of recognising the world's multiculturalism is of course progress, because it creates a climate conducive to the advance of cultures that yesterday were still wronged and humiliated, but this progress conceals two threats: firstly, the enormous energy and ambition of newly liberated cultures can be exploited by nationalists and racists to encourage war against Others; secondly, the rallying cry to develop one's own culture can be exploited to kindle ethnocentrism, xenophobia and enmity towards Others. Within the theory of independently developing cultures, in recognising their right to an inviolable identity – as the principle of multiculturalism is often interpreted – there may be a latent desire for separation, a denial of the need for and benefit of exchange, there may be arrogance and loathing for Others.

Taking part in a multicultural world demands a strong, mature sense of identity. How can it be established and confirmed? In Europe we define it through symbols with which we identify, such as a flag and a national anthem for instance. In African tradition, where identity was established through ties of kinship with a clan and a tribe, two Africans who met on the road would start their conversation with a long exchange of questions, in which both were trying to find out which tribe they were from and whether relations between their tribes were good or bad, because the quality and outcome of their meeting could depend on it.

Establishing identity, which is achieved inter alia by defining our relationship to Others, has been complicated in the past few decades for many reasons, and sometimes proves quite impossible. This is the result of a weakening of traditional cultural ties, caused by the migration of rural populations to cities, where a new type of identity is starting to be formed – a hybrid one, previously unprecedented on such a scale. At the beginning of the twentieth century 95 per cent of the world's population were peasants; today only half the world's citizens are peasants, and this class is gradually disappearing. The peasant class used to be the most faithful depositary of tradition and identity.

To sum up, we live in a multicultural world; in it Others are becoming someone other than they were yesterday, but who exactly is the topic for a debate that might take some time to resolve.

What about the history of relations between Europe and Others?

These Others, the non-Europeans, have made repeated attempts to conquer Europe, but in each case they were only partially successful. So it was for the Persians, later the Arabs, and finally the Mongols. (In the light of the debate ongoing today we do not know whether to regard the expansion of the Turks as the aggression of Others or as an intra-European conflict.)

In contrast, the conquests conducted by Europe are more numerous, far more effective and much bloodier. We only have to mention the eastern invasion of Alexander the Great, a few Crusades, the genocidal conquest of America by the Spanish, the 300-year depopulation of Africa by slave traders, and the colonial expansions of Britain, France, the Netherlands and so on, into extra-European continents.

Thus the mutual balance is tragic and sets a pessimistic tone, but we must not allow it to have a discouraging effect on us. On the contrary, firstly it is crucial to keep remembering and talking about Others, because today they are important players on the world stage. Secondly, though it is hard to prove that history teaches us about life, we must remember the unfortunate balance of our relations with Others, because just as a bad childhood leaves its marks on the whole of a person's later life, so a bad historical memory has an effect on later relations between societies.

Earlier I spoke of the eras when European thought tried to build bridges of understanding with Others. Referring to these efforts and carrying on with them is not just an ethical duty but also an urgent task for our time in a world where everything is so fragile and where there is so much demagogy, disorientation, fanaticism and bad will.

MY OTHER

The theme of the 'Stranger' or 'Other' has obsessed and fascinated me for a very long time. In 1956 I made my first long journey outside Europe (to India, Pakistan and Afghanistan), and from that moment to the present day I have been concerned with Third World issues, and thus with Asia, Africa and Latin America (though the term 'Third World' could also cover a considerable part of Europe and Oceania). I have spent most of my professional life in these parts, travelling and writing about the local people and their affairs.

I mention all this because here I would like to sketch – of necessity briefly – not a portrait of the Other in general, in abstraction, but a picture of *my* Other, the one I have met in native Indian villages in Bolivia, among nomads in the Sahara, or in the crowds bewailing the death of Khomeini on the streets of Teheran.

s world outlook, his view of the world, his
rs – his view of me, for example? After all,
an Other for me, I am an Other for him
too.

The first thing one notices is my Other's sensitivity
to colour, skin colour. Colour takes top place on the
scale according to which he will divide and judge
people. You can live your whole life without thinking,
without wondering about the fact that you are black,
yellow or white, until you cross the border of your own
racial zone. At once there is tension, at once we feel
like Others surrounded by *other* Others. How often in
Uganda I was touched by children who went on looking
at their fingers for a long time after to see if they had
gone white! The same mechanism, or reflex even, of
identifying and judging according to skin colour also
used to work inside me. In the Cold War years, when
there was an inexorable ideological division in force
between East and West, demanding of people on both
sides of the Iron Curtain a mutual dislike, or even
hatred – as a correspondent from an Eastern bloc
country somewhere out in the jungle of Zaire, I would
happily throw myself into the embrace of someone
from the West, and thus my 'class enemy', an
'imperialist', because that 'devious exploiter' and 'war-
monger' was simply and above all *white*. Must I add

how greatly ashamed I was of this weakness, but that at the same time I did not know how to resist it?

The second component of my Other's world outlook will be nationalism. As the American professor John Lukacs so aptly observed not long ago, at the close of the twentieth century nationalism proved to be the strongest of all the 'isms' known to contemporary man. Sometimes this nationalism has a paradoxical nature, for instance when it appears in those African countries where there are not yet any nations. There are no nations, but there is nationalism (or, as some sociologists maintain, sub-nationalism). The nationalist treats his nation, and in the case of Africa, his state, as the highest value, and all others as something inferior (and often deserving contempt). Nationalism, like racism, is a tool for identifying and classifying that is used by my Other at any opportunity. It is a crude, primitive tool that oversimplifies and trivialises one's image of the Other, because for the nationalist the person of the Other has just one single feature – national affiliation. It does not matter if someone is young or old, clever or stupid, good or bad – the only thing that counts is whether he or she is Armenian or Turkish, British or Irish, Moroccan or Algerian. When I live in that world of inflamed nationalisms, I have no name, no profession and no age – I am purely and simply a Pole. In Mexico my neighbours call me 'El Polaco', and the air hostess in Yakutsk summons me to board the plane by shouting 'Polsha!' Among small, scattered nations, such as the Armenians, there is a phenomenal capacity to see the map of the world as a network of points inhabited by concentrations of one's own compatriots, be it one single family or one single person. The dangerous feature of nationalism is that an inseparable part of it is hatred for an Other. The degree of this hatred varies, but its presence is inevitable.

The third component of my Other's world outlook is religion. Religious belief will feature here on two levels, so to speak – on the level of an ill-defined, non-verbalised faith in the existence and presence of transcendence, a Driving Force, a Supreme Being, God (I am often asked, 'Mr Kapuściński, do you believe in God?', and what I reply will have immense influence on everything that happens thereafter); and on the level of religion as an institution and as a social or even political force. I want to talk about the second instance. My Other is a creature who believes deeply in the existence of an extra-corporeal, extra-material world. Yet that has always been the case. What is characteristic of the present day, however, is the kind of religious renascence that is apparent in many countries. The most dynamically developing religion today is undoubtedly Islam. It is curious that everywhere – and this is regardless of the kind of religion – where a revival of religious fervour occurs, the revival has a reactionary, conservative, fundamental character.

So here is my Other. If fate brings him into contact with some Other – Other to him – he will find three features of that Other the most important: race, nationality and religion. I have been trying to find a common factor in these features, to discover what links them. It is that each one of them carries a huge emotional charge, so big that from time to time my Other is incapable of controlling it, and then it comes to conflict, to a clash, to slaughter, to war. My Other is a very emotional person. That is why the world he lives in is a powder keg rolling dangerously towards the fire.

My Other is a non-white person. How many of them are there? Today, 80 per cent of the world is non-white.

Occupied with the fight between East and West, between democracy and totalitarianism, not all of us were aware, and not all at once, that *the map of the world had changed*. In the first half of the twentieth century this map was arranged on the principles of a pyramid. At the top were historical subjects: the great colonial powers, the white man's states. This arrangement broke down before our eyes and in our lifetime, as more than a hundred new – at least formally independent – states inhabited by three-quarters of humanity appeared on the historical arena almost over-night. And so here is the new map of the world, colourful, multicoloured, very rich and complex. Let us note that if we compare the map of our world from the 1930s with the map from the 1980s, we get two completely different images of it. But in fact, the relationship between these two images is never static – it is undergoing constant change, constant dynamic and unstoppable evolution. In the latest history, the history that is happening right now, our Third World Others are gaining ever greater and ever more meaningful subjectivity. That is the first thing, and secondly, there is an invasion happening (a demographic one, to earn money, but it is an invasion) of representatives of the Third World into developed countries. It is estimated that by the mid-twenty-first century people from Asia and Latin America will constitute more than half the population of the United States.

More and more emigrants from Ireland and Norway, and more and more from Ecuador and Thailand, will move about the world with American passports in their pockets.

How prepared are we, the citizens of Europe, for this change? Not very, I'm afraid to say. We treat the Other above all as a stranger (yet the Other does not have to mean a stranger), as the representative of a separate species, but the most crucial point is that we treat him as a *threat*.

Does modern literature help to break down these prejudices, our ignorance or our plain indifference? Once again, I don't think it does much. I looked through the French literary awards for the past year, and did not find a single book with something to say about the widely understood modern world. There were love triangles, father–daughter conflict, a young couple's failed life together – things that are certainly important and interesting. But I was struck by the disdainful attitude towards the whole new trend in literature, just as fascinating, whose representatives are trying to show us the modern cultures, ideas and behaviour of people who live in different geographical latitudes and who believe in different gods from us, but who do actually constitute part of the great human family to which we all belong. I am thinking for example of *The Innocent Anthropologist* by Nigel Barley, of Colin Thubron's superbly written book *Behind the Wall* or Bruce Chatwin's excellent *Songlines*. These books do not win prizes, they are not even noticed, because – in some people's opinions – they are not so-called real literature.

On the other hand so-called real literature isolates itself from the problems and conflicts experienced by billions of our *Fremde*.[7] For example, one of the greatest dramas of the modern world, a drama particularly acute

7. Aliens, newcomers (German).

for America, was the Iranian revolution, the overthrow of the Shah, the fate of the hostages and so on. To my amazement, in the course of the dozen or more months when these events were happening I did not meet a single American writer in Iran, nor in fact a single writer from Europe. How can it be possible, I wondered in Teheran, for such a great historical shock, such an unusual clash of civilisations, not to stir any interest among the world's writers? Of course it is not that they should immediately rush off en masse to the latest trouble spot, to the Persian Gulf – but the fact that literature can completely ignore a world drama being played out before our very eyes, leaving it entirely up to the television cameras and sound operators to tell the story of major incidents, is to me a symptom of a deep crisis on the front line between history and literature, a symptom of literature's help-lessness in the face of modern world events.

So, despite an entirely new map of the world, researching, fathoming, interpreting and describing the philosophies and existence, the thinking and way of life of three-quarters of the world's population still remains – as in the nineteenth century – in the hands of a narrow group of specialists: anthropologists, ethnographers, tra-vellers and journalists.

The Stranger, the Other in his Third World incarnation (and so the most numerous individual on our planet), is still treated as the object of research, but has not yet become our partner, jointly responsible for the fate of the planet on which we live.

For me the world has always been a great Tower of Babel. However, it is a tower in which God has mixed not just the languages but also the cultures and customs, passions and interests, and whose inhabitant He has made into an ambivalent creature combining the Self and non-Self, himself and the Other, his own and the alien.

THE OTHER IN THE GLOBAL VILLAGE

Among many questions taken up by professor of philosophy Father Józef Tischner in his inquiries there are also reflections on the subject of the Other – the other person whom we encounter, with whom we come into contact or take up the thread of communication.[8] Tischner is one of the Polish thinkers known to me who discussed and developed issues concerning the Other at length and in a very profound way. What exactly are the significance, importance and relevance of these issues?

In the field of philosophical studies the first half of the twentieth century is dominated by the ontology and

8. Józef Tischner (1931–2000) was an eminent Polish priest and philosopher. The first chaplain of the trade union Solidarity, he was an exceptional moral authority and one of the most admired figures in Poland, both within the opposition to Communism and after the 1989 restoration of independence. His two main works, in which he explained his original philosophical concepts, were *The Philosophy of Drama* (*Filozofia dramatu*, 1998) and *The Controversy over Human Existence* (*Spór o istnienie człowieka*, 1998).

epistemology of Husserl and Heidegger. But neither of them puts ethics in first place. Meanwhile the experiences of the past century, with their tragic consequences for mankind and its culture, quite naturally make it necessary to take on these particular issues. Because in the first decades of the last century two new phenomena emerge on European ground that are previously unknown to history – the first is the birth of mass society, while the second is the rise of totalitarian systems that threaten the very essence of humanity – fascism and communism.

The birth and relationships between these two phenomena and processes rivet the attention of the thinkers and writers of that era – José Ortega y Gasset, Erich Fromm, Hannah Arendt, Theodor Adorno and many others. They try to understand the astounding world that has attacked them from all directions, they try to fathom, comprehend and define it. Soon the key word to describe it is the adjective 'mass'. Thus there is mass culture and mass hysteria, mass tastes (or rather lack of taste) and mass paranoia, mass enslavement, and finally mass murder. The only hero on the world stage is the crowd, and the main feature of this crowd, this mass, is anonymity, impersonality, lack of identity, lack of a face. The individual is lost in this crowd, the mass has engulfed him, and the waters of the lake have closed over him. To use Gabriel Marcel's term, he has become 'the nameless, anonymous person in a fragmentary state'.

The critical angle on this state of affairs produced a series of brilliant works attempting to show human destiny in a generalising form – as the experience of a community and as a jointly endured drama. Of a very large number of titles, here we could mention for example *The Revolt of the Masses*, *The Lonely Crowd* or *The Origins of Totalitarianism*.

However, if we follow the analyses, observations and theories of these thinkers, there comes a point where we start to sense a deficiency. In the course of their reasoning and syntheses we find there is an important link missing, which is the individual, the *specific person* distinguished from the mass, the specific Self – and the specific Other, as according to the claims of the philosophers of dialogue, I the Self can exist as a defined being *only in relation to*; in relation to the Other, when he appears on the horizon of my existence, giving me meaning and establishing my role.

In *The Philosophy of Drama* Tischner wrote:

At the start of the origin of awareness of the *self* lies the presence of *you*, and perhaps even the presence of a more general *we*. Only in dialogue, in argument, in opposition, and also in aspiring towards a new community is awareness of *my self* created, as a *self-contained being*, separate from another. I know that I am, because I know *another* is.[9]

It is out of the need to generalise this experience that the philosophy of dialogue arises.

The philosophy of dialogue is the movement, orientation or trend that tries to address the issues of man – the Self, and extremely crucially, *his relations with another person*, with the Other. This enriching reorientation from issues that are strictly ontological to broader ethical issues, and this radical application of philosophical thought to man as an individual, separate, incomparable and unique being, are also plainly evident in the work of Józef Tischner, where thinking about an encounter between the Self and the Other – in fact already emphasised in *Thinking According to Values* – is the leading theme in *The Philosophy of Drama*, first published in 1998.

In our modern times this trend has been formed and most consistently developed by Martin Buber and Franz Rosenzweig, Gabriel Marcel and the philosopher most often quoted by Tischner, Emmanuel Lévinas.

9. J. Tischner, *Filozofia Dramatu*, trans. A. Lloyd-Jones Krakow: Znak, 2006, p. 219.

We can discern the specific roots of the philosophy of dialogue or (as we also say) the philosophy of encounter or the philosophy of the Other – and especially its statements suggesting that the way to God leads via the Other, and that we are able to see His countenance in the face of the Other – in the ancient anthropomorphic era, when human imagination had not yet marked out the border between the world of gods and men, and when the divinity was conceived as having the likeness of man or vice versa.

Józef Tischner practised the philosophy of the Other with passion and perspicacity to the very end of his earthly journey. In his tireless promotion of its beliefs and principles – and this is true today in particular, in the times we live in – lie profound humanity and genuine heroism. And that is why, apart from strictly academic values, it is worth so much that it bravely and openly comes out in defence of another person, in defence of the Other, in a world that so often yields to the temptations of selfishness and greedy consumerism.

The great merit of this philosophy is that it talks about the individual person at all, about each single one as significant in himself, and that it keeps on reminding us of his existence and articulation. In all our postmodern commotion, in our confusion of languages, a strong, clear voice raising such qualities as identity, respect, noticing and esteeming another – the Other – is invaluable. But that is not the end of it; in developing and enriching the themes that appear in Emmanuel Lévinas's philosophy, particularly in *Totality and Infinity*, Tischner says that the Self not only has to relate to the Other, but must assume responsibility for him and be prepared to bear the consequences of such a decision, such an attitude. Is there a Christian act of sacrifice in this? Yes – of sacrifice, renunciation and humility.

The philosophy of encounter has so far considered the question of the Other and our relationship with him, our attitude to him, generally, within a first-hand, direct situation and within the sphere of the same culture. This philosophical trend has yet to enter the field of inquiries into the relationship between the Self and the Other when one of the sides belongs to another race, religion or culture. To what extent will this complicate the flow of our reflections, making them more elaborate, difficult and ambiguous?

This is extremely important today, when we live in a multicultural world, and advances in communications are making the multicultural nature of our modern world more and more obvious and ubiquitous. In fact, our planet has always been multicultural – since time immemorial the people on it have spoken different languages and believed in different gods, but the world's destiny developed in such a way that for the past five centuries European culture or civilisation has dominated us, and as a result, in saying 'we', we understood – 'we, all people', though in reality we only meant us, the Europeans. Nowadays, however, we are already irrevocably entering an era when the unambiguous equation 'we = Europeans' as a synonym for all the people in the world is being questioned by ongoing historical changes.

As a consequence of these changes, other cultures, which are very numerous, yet which until now have been dominated or marginalised, have awoken, come to life and started to demand an equal place at the world's round table. They are ambitious and dynamic, and at the same time have a strongly developed sense of values. In these efforts to obtain a new place under the sun and acknowledgement of proper rights for the Other, the philosophers and thinkers who belong to those rising cultures will be able to gain inspiration from the thoughts produced by Tischner, the Kraków-based cleric and thinker from the village of Łopuszna.

Tischner and other dialogists try to sow a salutary concern in us, to tell us about the existence, and even the close presence of the Other, the necessity to feel responsible for him – moreover to recognise that this responsibility is a weighty ethical imperative. What courage it takes even to raise this topic and point out its transcendent dimension at a time when in modern culture the dominant attitude involves limiting and enclosing oneself in one's private, egotistical 'me', within a tightly isolated circle where one can satisfy one's own urges and consumer whims. Resisting the temptations and diktat of consumerism – the spirit of responsibility for the Other, that is where Tischner sees a person's duty, or even obligation.

Reflecting on the Other prompts Józef Tischner to consider the nature and content of an encounter between the Self and the Other – an encounter that, as he very often stresses, should be an important event. And so we should internally prepare for this encounter, because it should be the opposite of our usual, indifferent way of passing each other in the crowd. This encounter is an experience worth remembering, and might be a profound one. And again Tischner warns us that when meeting the Other we should remain fully aware of the importance of this fact, aware of its place and role in the private, individual, spiritual history of our own Self. With this warning he wants to take the nature, content and gravity of interpersonal relations, their meaning for us and their influence on us, a crucial step higher.

But what is the main content of the encounter? It is dialogue. In Tischner's final texts certain phrases keep recurring, such as 'dialogical openness', 'dialogical perspective', 'dialogical awareness', 'dialogical plane', etc. As Lévinas defines it: 'Man is a creature that talks.' And so we have dialogue. The aim of this dialogue is meant to be mutual understanding, while the aim of this understanding is to come closer to each other, and this understanding and coming closer are achieved by way of getting to know each other. What is the preliminary condition for this entire process, this equation? It is the *will* to become acquainted, the desire, the act of turning towards the Other, coming out to meet him, entering into conversation with him. However, in actual practice it turns out to be extremely difficult. Human experience shows that at the first moment, as a first reflex a person reacts to an Other with reserve and restraint, mistrust or plain reluctance, or even with hostility. In the broad course of history all of us human beings have inflicted too many blows on each other and caused each other too much pain for things to be otherwise. Hence entire civilisations have been characterised by this sense of alienation towards the Other. The Greeks called non-Greeks *barbaros*: those who speak gibberish and cannot be understood, so it is better to keep them at a distance – at a distance and in a state of humiliation. The Romans built a network of border fortifications against the Other, called *limes*. The Chinese called non-Chinese strangers from across the ocean *Yang-kwei*, meaning sea monsters, and did their best to keep them at arm's length.

And in our times? What about the arrogance of one group towards the cultures and religions of others? And the archipelagos of all sorts of ghettoes and camps spread about our planet? All manner of walls and barriers, ditches and entanglements? How much of it there is everywhere, on all continents! What a difficult challenge advances in communications have become in recent decades. On the one hand they are definitely bringing us closer to each other, but are they really bringing us *together*? Between person and person, between the Self and the Other, a technological intermediary has been introduced – an electrical spark, an electronic impulse, a network, a link, a satellite. The Hindi word *upanishada* means to sit near, to be near. The Self has been brought to the Other not only by words, but also by being close, by direct contact, by being together. Nothing is capable of taking the place of this experience.

The paradoxical nature of the media situation goes further. On the one hand the media are becoming more globalised, but on the other they are becoming shallower, more incoherent and confused. The more contact a person has with the media, the more he complains of feeling lost and isolated. In the early 1960s, Marshall

McLuhan coined the term 'the global village' when television was still at an embryonic stage. McLuhan was a Catholic with great missionary zeal, who imagined that the new medium would make us all brothers living in one community of faith. This expression of his, repeated today without a second thought, has proved to be one of the greatest mistakes of modern culture, because the essence of a village depends on the fact that its inhabitants know each other well, commune with each other and share a common fate. Meanwhile nothing of the kind can be said of society on our planet, which is more like the anonymous crowd at a major airport, a crowd of people rushing along in haste, mutually indifferent and ignorant.

It is only against this sort of background that we feel all the more distinctly the profound humanity, ardour and hope of Józef Tischner's teaching on the Self and the Other as the basis for harmony on Earth.

*ENCOUNTERING THE OTHER
AS THE CHALLENGE OF THE
TWENTY-FIRST CENTURY*

When I stop to think about the journeys I have been making around the world for a very long time now, sometimes I feel that the most worrying problems did not involve borders and frontiers, practical difficulties and threats, so much as a frequently recurring uncertainty about the form, quality and course of an encounter with Others, with the other people whom I would come across somewhere along the way, because I knew that a lot, sometimes everything, would depend on it. Each encounter of this kind was an unknown quantity – how would it go? How would it develop? What would be the conclusion?

Of course questions of this sort are eternal. An encounter with another person, with other people, has always been a universal, fundamental experience for our species. The archaeologists tell us that the first human groups were small family-tribes numbering thirty to fifty individuals. If such a society were bigger, it would be hard for it to move about quickly and ably. If it were smaller, it would be harder for it to defend itself effectively, to fight for survival.

And so our small family-tribe is moving about in search of food, when suddenly it comes across another family-tribe. What an important moment in the history of the world, what a major discovery – the discovery that there are other people in the world too! For until now a member of the primitive group we have mentioned could have lived in the conviction that as he moves about within the circle of his thirty to fifty relatives he knows all the people on Earth. Meanwhile it turns out he did not, and that there are other, similar creatures in the world, other people!

How should he behave in the face of this revelation? How should he proceed? What decision should he make? Furiously attack the people encountered? Pass them by indifferently and keep going? Or try to get to know them and communicate with them?

The same choice that a group of our ancestors found themselves facing thousands of years ago still stands before us today, and with the same unflagging intensity: a choice that is just as basic and categorical as then. How should we relate to Others? What attitude should we take to them?

It may be that it comes to a duel, to conflict, to war – evidence of this sort of incident is preserved by all the archives and marked by the fields of innumerable battles and the remains of ruins scattered worldwide. They are all proof of man's defeat – of the fact that he was unable or unwilling to come to an understanding with Others. The literature of every country in every era has taken this situation as its theme, offering endless variety and atmosphere.

However, it may also be that instead of attacking and fighting, the family-tribe we have been following decides to isolate itself from Others, to separate and fence itself off. In time, as a result of this sort of attitude, objects start to appear that are all based on a similar intention, such as the Great Wall of China, the towers and gates of Babylon, the Roman limes or the stone walls of the Incas.

Fortunately, there is evidence of a third way of proceeding that is familiar to human experience. This is proof of cooperation – the remains of marketplaces, the remains of harbours, the sites of agoras and shrines, where the seats of old universities and academies are still in evidence, or the traces of trade routes have survived, such as the Silk Road, the Amber or the Saharan. In these places people encountered each other at every turn, exchanged thoughts, ideas and goods, traded and did business, made alliances and unions, found common aims and values. The different, other person ceased to be a synonym for a stranger and an enemy, a threat or a deadly evil. Each person discovered in himself at least a small particle of that Other, believed in it and lived in this conviction.

And so the three possibilities I have mentioned have always stood before man whenever he has encountered an Other: he could choose war, he could fence himself in behind a wall, or he could start up a dialogue.

Over the course of history man has never stopped wavering between these options; depending on the situation and culture he makes now one, now another choice; we can see that he is changeable in these choices, that he does not always feel certain, and is not always standing on firm ground.

It is hard to justify wars; I think everyone loses them, because it is a defeat for the human being. It exposes his inability to come to terms, to empathise with the Other, to be kind and reasonable, because in this case the encounter with the Other always ends tragically, in a drama of blood and death.

The idea that prompted man to build great walls and vast moats, to surround himself with them and isolate himself from others, has in modern times been given the name of the doctrine of apartheid. This concept has been wrongly limited to the politics of the now defunct regime of whites in

South Africa, for in fact apartheid was already practised in ancient times. In simple terms it is a view whose adherents proclaim that anyone may live as he wishes, as long as he is at a distance from me, if he does not belong to my race, religion and culture. But if only that were all it was about, because in fact here we are dealing with a doctrine of structural permanent inequality dividing humankind.

The myths of many tribes and peoples include a belief that only we are human, the members of our clan, our society, and that Others – all Others – are subhuman, or not human at all.

How different the image of the same Other is in the era of anthropomorphic beliefs, in other words those where the gods can take on human form and behave like people. For in those days no one could be sure if an approaching traveller, nomad or stranger were a man or a god resembling a man. This uncertainty, this intriguing ambivalence is one of the sources of the culture of hospitality, which recommends showing every form of kindness to newcomers.

The Polish poet Cyprian Norwid writes about this in his introduction to *The Odyssey*, as he considers the reasons for the hospitality that Odysseus encountered on his return journey to Ithaca:

There in every beggar and foreign wanderer the first suspicion was whether or not he might be God . . . It was impossible to host anyone without first asking: who is this stranger? But only because one respected the divinity in him, did it come down to human questions, and that was called hospitality, which was why it was counted among religious practices and virtues. There was no 'last person' among Homer's Greeks! He was always the first, that is, divine.[10]

In this Greek understanding of culture described by Norwid, things reveal their new, sympathetic meanings. Doors and gates are not just to shut ourselves away from Others, but can also be opened to them, to invite them in as guests. The road does not have to serve enemy armies – it can also be a route along which one of the gods comes to us, dressed as a pilgrim. Thanks to this sort of interpretation we start to circulate in a world that is not just richer and more diverse, but also more friendly towards us, a world where we ourselves will want to meet the Other.

Emmanuel Lévinas calls an encounter with the Other an 'event', or even a 'fundamental event'; this is the most important test, the most far-reaching horizon of experience. As we know, Lévinas belonged to the group of dialogist philosophers that included Martin

10. C. Norwid, *Pisma Wszystkie*, vol. III, ed. J. W. Gomulicki, trans. A. Lloyd-Jones, Warsaw: Państwowy Instytut Wydawniczy, 1971, pp. 673–96.

Buber, Ferdinand Ebner and Gabriel Marcel (later Józef Tischner joined their group too); they developed the idea of the Other – as a single, unique being – in more or less central opposition to two phenomena that appeared in the twentieth century. These were: the birth of mass society that erased the identity of the individual; and the rise of destructive totalitarian ideologies. These philosophers tried to protect the value they considered the greatest – the human individual: me, you, the Other, Others – from the effects of the masses and totalitarianism that eliminate all human identity (hence they disseminated the concept of the Other to underline the difference between one person and another, the difference of having irreplaceable, non-exchangeable features).

Where relations towards the Other and Others are concerned, these philosophers rejected the war route as leading to destruction, and criticised the attitude of indifference or isolation behind a wall, proclaiming instead the need – more than that, the ethical duty – to approach, to be open and friendly.

Within the sphere of this sort of thinking and belief, this kind of enquiry and reflection, this sort of attitude, the great research of a student, and later doctoral graduate of the Jagiellonian University is born and develops – the work of Polish Academy member Bronisław Malinowski.

Malinowski's problem was how to get close to the Other if he is not a purely abstract creature, but a specific person belonging to a different race, with his own beliefs and values that are different from ours, his own culture and customs.

Let us note that the concept of 'the Other' is usually defined from the white, European point of view. Nowadays, however, as I walk through a village in the mountains of Ethiopia, a gang of children runs after me, pointing at me in amusement and shouting: 'Faranji! Faranji!' That means 'foreigner', 'other', because to them I am an Other.

In this sense we are all in the same boat. Every one of us living on this planet is an Other in the view of Others – I am in their view, and they are in mine.

In Malinowski's era and the centuries preceding it the white man, the European, ventured beyond his own continent almost exclusively with the purpose of conquest – to gain control of new lands, capture slaves, trade or convert. These expeditions were often extremely bloody – the conquest of America by Columbus's people, and then by white settlers, the conquest of Africa, Asia and Australia.

Malinowski set off for the Pacific islands with a different purpose – he wanted to get to know the Other, to know his neighbours, customs and language, to see how he lived. He wanted to see and experience this thing for himself, in person, to experience it so that later he could bear witness.

Malinowski's project seems obvious, but it turns out to have been revolutionary, earth-shattering, because it exposed a weakness that appears in varying degrees in, or may simply be a trait of, every culture, involving the fact that one culture has problems understanding another, and that the people who belong to those cultures, their participants and bearers, have these problems.

Most notably, in his book *Coral Gardens* Malinowski claimed after arriving at the site of his research – the Trobriand Islands – that the whites who had been living there for years not only knew nothing about the local population and its culture, but had completely false images of them, typified by contempt and arrogance. And in defiance of all sorts of colonial habits, he pitched his tent in the middle of one of the local villages and settled in with the local population. What he experienced was not easy to endure. In his account, *A Diary in the Strict Sense of the Term*, he made more and more comments about his troubles, bad moods, moments of despair and even depression.

He paid a high price for breaking away from his own culture. That is why it is so important to have one's own, distinct identity, a sense of its strength, value and maturity. Only then can a man boldly confront another culture. Otherwise he will lurk in his hiding place, fearfully isolating himself from others. All the more since the Other is a looking glass in which I see myself, and in which I am observed – it is a mirror that unmasks and exposes me, something we would prefer to avoid.

It is interesting that while the First World War was going on in Malinowski's native Europe, the young anthropologist was focusing his research on the culture of exchange, the contacts and common rituals among the inhabitants of the Trobriand Islands, to which he devoted his wonderful book *Argonauts of the West Pacific*. He formulated an important thesis, so rarely perceived by others: that 'to judge something, you have to be there'. He came up with another thesis too, incredibly bold for those times, which is that there are no superior or inferior cultures – there are just different cultures, which satisfy the needs and expectations of their members in different ways. To him the other person, from another race and culture, is in fact an individual whose behaviour, just like that of every one of us, is typified by dignity, respect for recognised values and esteem for traditions and customs.

If Malinowski began his work at the moment when mass society was born, nowadays we are living in a period of transition from that mass society to a new, global one. A lot of things support this change: the electronic revolution, the incredible development of all sorts of communications, advances that make it much easier to get in touch and to move about, and also – as a result – transformations occurring in the consciousness of the youngest generations and within broadly understood culture.

How will this change our attitude – as the people of one culture – to people of another culture or other cultures? How will it influence relations between my Self and the Other within the sphere of my culture and beyond it? It is very hard to give an unambiguous, final answer, because we are talking about an ongoing process in which we ourselves are immersed, with no opportunity for the sort of detachment needed for reflection.

Lévinas considered relations between the Self and the Other within the sphere of a single, historically and racially homogeneous civilisation. Malinowski researched Melanesian tribes at a time when they still preserved their primitive state, undisturbed by the influences of Western technology, organisation and commerce.

Nowadays, however, that is more and more rarely possible. Culture is becoming increasingly hybrid and heterogeneous. Not long ago in Dubai I saw an astonishing sight – it was a girl walking along the seashore, definitely a Muslim. She was wearing tight jeans and a tight top, but at the same time her head, just her head, was covered by a dark chador so puritanically sealed that not even her eyes were visible.

Nowadays there are whole schools of philosophy, anthropology and literary criticism whose main focus is this process of hybridisation, combination and cultural transformation. This process is especially active in those regions where the borders of states used to be the borders of different cultures (such as the US-Mexican border), and also in gigantic mega-cities (such as São Paulo, New York or Singapore), where there is a mixed population representing a huge variety of cultures and races. Moreover, nowadays we say that the world has become multi-ethnic and multi-cultural, not because there are more of these societies and cultures than before, but because they are speaking ever louder, ever more independently and decisively demanding to be accepted and acknowledged, and to be given a place at the round table of nations.

The real challenge of our times, the encounter with the new Other, the racially and culturally Other, also derives from a broader historical context. The second half of the twentieth century was a time when two-thirds of the world's population were liberated from colonial dependency and became citizens of their own, at least nominally autonomous states. Gradually these people are starting to discover their own past, myths and roots, their own history, sense of identity and, of course, the pride resulting from it. They are starting to feel themselves masters and commanders of their own destiny, regarding with hatred any attempts to treat them purely as extras, as the background, as victims or passive objects of domination.

Today, our planet, inhabited for centuries by a narrow group of free people and broad ranks of the enslaved, is being filled with a rising number of nations and societies that have a growing sense of their own importance and separate value.

This process often occurs amid vast difficulties, conflicts and dramas.

Perhaps we are tending towards a world so completely new and different that the experience of history to date will prove inadequate for understanding it and being able to move about in it.

In any case the world we are entering is the Planet of Great Opportunity – not an unconditional opportunity, but one that is only open to those who take their tasks seriously, proving by this token that they take themselves seriously. It is a world that has the potential to give a lot, but also demands a lot, and where any attempt to take an easy shortcut is often a road to nowhere.

In it we shall constantly be encountering the new Other, who will gradually start to emerge from the chaos and confusion of modern life. It is possible that this

Other will be born out of an encounter between two opposing trends that form the culture of the modern world – one that is globalising our reality, and another that is preserving our dissimilarity, our differences, our uniqueness. He will be their son and heir, and that is why we should seek dialogue and communication with him. The experience of spending many years among distant Others has taught me that friendliness towards another human being is the only attitude that can touch a chord of humanity in him.

Who will this new Other be? What will our encounter be like? What shall we say to each other? And in what language? Will we be able to listen to each other? Understand each other? Will we jointly wish to refer to what – as Conrad puts it – 'speaks to our capacity for delight and wonder, to the sense of mystery surrounding our lives; to our sense of pity, and beauty, and pain; to the latent feeling of fellowship with all creation – and to the subtle but invincible conviction of solidarity that knits together the loneliness of innumerable hearts: to the solidarity in dreams, in joy, in sorrow, in aspirations, in illusions, in hope, in fear, which binds men to each other, which binds together all humanity – the dead to the living and the living to the unborn'?[11]

11. J. Conrad, Preface to *The Nigger of the 'Narcissus': A Tale of the Sea*, New York: W. W. Norton, 1979.

INDEX

INDEX

Radcliffe-Brown, Alfred, 30
Raynal, Guillaume, 25
Religion, 56–57, 70, 74
Renaissance, 38
The Revolt of the Masses (Ortega y Gasset), 67
Rivers, W. H. R., 30
Roman Empire, 20, 73, 81
Rosenzweig, Franz, 68
Rousseau, Jean-Jacques, 23
Russia, 23

Sahara
  nomads of the, 53
  trade routes of, 81
São Paulo, city of, 90
Sapir, Edward, 44
Sapir–Whorf hypothesis, 43
Science, 24
Scythians, 19
Self, Other in relation to, 8, 34, 61, 74
  Christian sacrifice and, 70
  culture and, 89
  dependence and, 67–68
  inclusion of Other in Self, 37
Siberia, 23
Silk Road trade route, 81
Simmel, Georg, 44
Singapore, 90

Skarga, Barbara, 36–37
Skin colour, 45, 54–55
Slavery/slave trade, 22, 25, 28
Socialism, 6
Songlines (Chatwin), 59
South Africa, 82–83
Soviet Union, 6, 45
Stalin, Joseph, 1
Swift, Jonathan, 23

Taylor, Charles, 21
Television, 15, 60, 75
Le temps et l'autre (Lévinas), 36
Thinking According to Values (Tischner), 68
Third World, 26, 33, 53, 58, 60–61
Thubron, Colin, 59
Tischner, Father Józef, 4, 8, 65, 69, 75
  dialogist philosophers and, 85
  on dialogue, 72–73
  The Philosophy of Drama, 65n8, 67–68
  on responsibility for the Other, 71–72
  Thinking According to Values, 68
Torah, 15
Totalitarianism, 8, 34, 57, 66, 85

99